Contents

Book Title	Crime/Horror	Classic	Romance	Fantasy/Sci-fi	Historical	Biography	[Personal Preference]	[Personal Preference]	[Personal Preference]
1									
2									
3									
4									
5									
6									
7									
8									
9									
10									
11									
12									
13									
14									
15									
16									
17									
18									
19									
20									
21									
22									
23									
24									
25									

Book Title	Crime/Horror	Classic	Romance	Fantasy/Sci-fi	Historical	Biography	[Personal Preference]	[Personal Preference]	[Personal Preference]
26									
27									
28									
29									
30									
31									
32									
33									
34									
35									
36									
37									
38									
39									
40									
41									
42									
43									
44									
45									
46									
47									
48									
49									
50									

Book Title	Crime/Horror	Classic	Romance	Fantasy/Sci-fi	Historical	Biography	[Personal Preference]	[Personal Preference]	[Personal Preference]
51									
52									
53									
54									
55									
56									
57									
58									
59									
60									
61									
62									
63									
64									
65									
66									
67									
68									
69									
70									
71									
72									
73									
74									
75									

Book Title	Crime/Horror	Classic	Romance	Fantasy/Sci-fi	Historical	Biography	[Personal Preference]	[Personal Preference]	[Personal Preference]
76									
77									
78									
79									
80									
81									
82									
83									
84									
85									
86									
87									
88									
89									
90									
91									
92									
93									
94									
95									
96									
97									
98									
99									
100									

Paperback ○   Hardback ○   e-book ○   Audiobook ○

1

Title:

Author: _____

Publisher: _____   Pub. date _____

Page count: _____

○ Fiction   ○ Non-fiction

  Genre: _____   Subject: _____

Dates
Started: 8/16/18
Finished: _____

Source
Bought ● Loaned ○
From: _____

My Review:
_____
_____
_____
_____
_____
_____
_____
_____
_____
_____
_____
_____
_____
_____

Great quotes from this book.

Inspiration Tree

Why I read it?
_____
↓
It inspired me to
(read/learn/visit)?
_____
_____
↓
Who will I
recommend it to?
_____

✳ Ratings ✳

Plot: 1 2 3 4 5
Characters:
1 2 3 4 5
Ease of reading:
1 2 3 4 5
Overall
☹ 😐 🙂

2

Paperback ○   Hardback ○   e-book ○   Audiobook ○

Title:

Dates
Started: _____
Finished: _____

Source
Bought ○   Loaned ○
From: _____

Author: _____
Publisher: _____   Pub. date _____
Page count: _____
○ Fiction   ○ Non-fiction
   Genre: _____   Subject: _____

My Review:
_____
_____
_____
_____
_____
_____
_____
_____
_____
_____
_____
_____
_____

Inspiration Tree

Why I read it?
_____
↓
It inspired me to
(read/learn/visit)?
_____
_____
↓
Who will I
recommend it to?
_____

✳ Ratings ✳

Plot: 1 2 3 4 5
Characters:
1 2 3 4 5
Ease of reading:
1 2 3 4 5
Overall
☹ 😐 😊

Great quotes from this book:

Paperback ○   Hardback ○   e-book ○   Audiobook ○

3

Title:

Author: _____

Publisher: _____ Pub. date _____

Page count: _____

○ Fiction   ○ Non-fiction
   Genre: _____   Subject: _____

Dates
Started: _____
Finished: _____

Source
Bought ○ Loaned ○
From: _____

My Review: _____
_____
_____
_____
_____
_____
_____
_____
_____
_____
_____
_____
_____
_____

Inspiration Tree

Why I read it?
_____
↓
It inspired me to
(read/learn/visit)?
_____
_____
↓
Who will I
recommend it to?
_____

⚹ Ratings ⚹

Plot: 1 2 3 4 5
Characters:
1 2 3 4 5
Ease of reading:
1 2 3 4 5
Overall
☹ 😐 ☺

Great quotes from this book:

4

Title:

Dates
Started: _____
Finished: _____

Source
Bought O   Loaned O
From: _____

Author: _____
Publisher: _____   Pub. date _____
Page count: _____
O Fiction   O Non-fiction
   Genre: _____   Subject: _____

Inspiration Tree

Why I read it?
_____
↓
It inspired me to
(read/learn/visit)?
_____
↓
Who will I
recommend it to?
_____

My Review:
_____
_____
_____
_____
_____
_____
_____
_____
_____
_____
_____
_____

✳ Ratings ✳

Plot: 1 2 3 4 5
Characters:
1 2 3 4 5
Ease of reading:
1 2 3 4 5
Overall
☹ 😐 🙂

Great quotes from this book:

Paperback ○   Hardback ○   e-book ○   Audiobook ○

5

Title:

Author: _____

Publisher: _____   Pub. date _____

Page count: _____

○ Fiction   ○ Non-fiction
  Genre: _____   Subject: _____

Dates
Started: _____
Finished: _____

Source
Bought ○ Loaned ○
From: _____

My Review: _____
_____
_____
_____
_____
_____
_____
_____
_____
_____
_____
_____
_____
_____
_____
_____

Great quotes from this book:

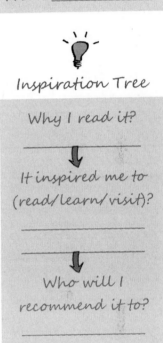

Inspiration Tree

Why I read it?
_____
↓
It inspired me to
(read/learn/visit)?
_____
↓
Who will I
recommend it to?
_____

✳ Ratings ✳

Plot: 1 2 3 4 5
Characters:
1 2 3 4 5
Ease of reading:
1 2 3 4 5
Overall
☹ 😐 ☺

6

Title:

Author:

Publisher: _____   Pub. date _____

Page count: _____

○ Fiction   ○ Non-fiction
  Genre: _____   Subject: _____

Dates
Started: _____
Finished: _____

Source
Bought ○   Loaned ○
From: _____

Inspiration Tree

Why I read it?
_____
↓
It inspired me to
(read/learn/visit)?
_____
_____
↓
Who will I
recommend it to?
_____

✳ Ratings ✳

Plot: 1 2 3 4 5
Characters:
1 2 3 4 5
Ease of reading:
1 2 3 4 5
Overall
☹ 😐 ☺

My Review: _____
_____
_____
_____
_____
_____
_____
_____
_____
_____
_____
_____

Great quotes from this book:

Paperback ○   Hardback ○   e-book ○   Audiobook ○

7

Title:

Author: _____

Publisher: _____ Pub. date _____

Page count: _____

○ Fiction   ○ Non-fiction

  Genre: _____   Subject: _____

Dates
Started: _____
Finished: _____

Source
Bought ○ Loaned ○
From: _____

My Review: _____

_____

_____

_____

_____

_____

_____

_____

_____

_____

_____

_____

_____

_____

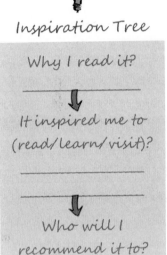

Inspiration Tree

Why I read it?
_____
↓
It inspired me to
(read/learn/visit)?
_____
_____
↓
Who will I
recommend it to?
_____

✳ Ratings ✳

Plot: 1 2 3 4 5
Characters:
1 2 3 4 5
Ease of reading:
1 2 3 4 5
Overall
☹ 😐 🙂

Great quotes from this book:

8

Title:

Author:

Publisher: _____   Pub. date _____

Page count: _____

○ Fiction

Genre: _____

○ Non-fiction

Subject: _____

Dates

Started: _____

Finished: _____

Source

Bought ○   Loaned ○

From: _____

Inspiration Tree

Why I read it?

_____

↓

It inspired me to
(read/learn/visit)?

_____

_____

↓

Who will I
recommend it to?

_____

✴ Ratings ✴

Plot: 1 2 3 4 5

Characters:
1 2 3 4 5

Ease of reading:
1 2 3 4 5

Overall

☹ 😐 🙂

My Review:

_____
_____
_____
_____
_____
_____
_____
_____
_____
_____
_____
_____
_____
_____

Great quotes from this book:

Paperback ○   Hardback ○   e-book ○   Audiobook ○

9

Title:

Author: _____

Publisher: _____   Pub. date _____

Page count: _____

○ Fiction   ○ Non-fiction

   Genre: _____   Subject: _____

Dates
Started: _____
Finished: _____

Source
Bought ○ Loaned ○
From: _____

My Review: _____

_____

_____

_____

_____

_____

_____

_____

_____

_____

_____

_____

_____

_____

Inspiration Tree

Why I read it?
_____
↓
It inspired me to
(read/learn/visit)?
_____
_____
↓
Who will I
recommend it to?
_____

✳ Ratings ✳

Plot: 1 2 3 4 5
Characters:
1 2 3 4 5
Ease of reading:
1 2 3 4 5
Overall
☹ 😐 🙂

Great quotes from this book:

Paperback ○   Hardback ○   e-book ○   Audiobook ○

Title:

Dates
Started: _____
Finished: _____

Source
Bought ○   Loaned ○
From: _____

Inspiration Tree

Why I read it?
_____
↓
It inspired me to
(read/learn/visit)?
_____
_____
↓
Who will I
recommend it to?
_____

✳ Ratings ✳

Plot: 1 2 3 4 5
Characters:
1 2 3 4 5
Ease of reading:
1 2 3 4 5
Overall
☹ 😐 🙂

Author: _____
Publisher: _____   Pub. date _____
Page count: _____
○ Fiction   ○ Non-fiction
   Genre: _____   Subject: _____

My Review: ....

_____
_____
_____
_____
_____
_____
_____
_____
_____
_____
_____
_____

Great quotes from this book:

Paperback ○   Hardback ○   e-book ○   Audiobook ○

11

Title:

Author: _____

Publisher: _____ Pub. date _____

Page count: _____

○ Fiction   ○ Non-fiction

Genre: _____   Subject: _____

Dates
Started: _____
Finished: _____

Source
Bought ○ Loaned ○

From: _____

My Review: _____

_____

_____

_____

_____

_____

_____

_____

_____

_____

_____

_____

_____

Inspiration Tree

Why I read it?
_____
↓
It inspired me to
(read/learn/visit)?
_____
_____
↓
Who will I
recommend it to?
_____

Great quotes from this book:

✹ Ratings ✹

Plot: 1 2 3 4 5
Characters:
1 2 3 4 5
Ease of reading:
1 2 3 4 5
Overall
☹ 😐 ☺

12

Paperback ○   Hardback ○   e-book ○   Audiobook ○

Title:

Dates
Started: _____
Finished: _____

Source
Bought ○   Loaned ○
From: _____

Author: _____

Publisher: _____   Pub. date _____

Page count: _____

○ Fiction   ○ Non-fiction
  Genre: _____   Subject: _____

💡

Inspiration Tree

Why I read it?
_____
⬇
It inspired me to
(read/learn/visit)?
_____
_____
⬇
Who will I
recommend it to?
_____

My Review: _____

_____

_____

_____

_____

_____

_____

_____

_____

_____

_____

_____

_____

✳ Ratings ✳

Plot: 1 2 3 4 5
Characters:
1 2 3 4 5
Ease of reading:
1 2 3 4 5
Overall
☹ 😐 🙂

Great quotes from this book:

Paperback ○   Hardback ○   e-book ○   Audiobook ○

13

Title:

Author: _____

Publisher: _____ Pub. date _____

Page count: _____

○ Fiction   ○ Non-fiction

  Genre: _____   Subject: _____

Dates
Started: _____
Finished: _____

Source
Bought ○   Loaned ○
From: _____

My Review: _____

_____

_____

_____

_____

_____

_____

_____

_____

_____

_____

_____

_____

_____

_____

Great quotes from this book:

Inspiration Tree

Why I read it?
_____

It inspired me to
(read/learn/visit)?
_____
_____

Who will I
recommend it to?
_____

✳ Ratings ✳

Plot: 1 2 3 4 5
Characters:
1 2 3 4 5
Ease of reading:
1 2 3 4 5
Overall
☹ 😐 🙂

14

Title:

Dates

Started: _____

Finished: _____

Source

Bought ○   Loaned ○

From: _____

Author: _____

Publisher: _____   Pub. date _____

Page count: _____

○ Fiction   ○ Non-fiction

  Genre: _____   Subject: _____

My Review: _____

_____

_____

_____

_____

_____

_____

_____

_____

_____

_____

_____

_____

Inspiration Tree

Why I read it?

_____

It inspired me to
(read/learn/visit)?

_____

_____

Who will I
recommend it to?

_____

✳ Ratings ✳

Plot: 1 2 3 4 5

Characters:
1 2 3 4 5

Ease of reading:
1 2 3 4 5

Overall

☹ 😐 🙂

Great quotes from this book:

Paperback ○   Hardback ○   e-book ○   Audiobook ○

15

Title:

Author: _____

Publisher: _____   Pub. date _____

Page count: _____

○ Fiction   ○ Non-fiction

  Genre: _____   Subject: _____

Dates
Started: _____
Finished: _____

Source
Bought ○   Loaned ○
From: _____

My Review: _____

_____

_____

_____

_____

_____

_____

_____

_____

_____

_____

_____

_____

_____

Inspiration Tree

Why I read it?
_____
↓
It inspired me to
(read/learn/visit)?
_____
_____
↓
Who will I
recommend it to?
_____

✳ Ratings ✳

Plot: 1 2 3 4 5
Characters:
1 2 3 4 5
Ease of reading:
1 2 3 4 5
Overall
☹ 😐 🙂

Great quotes from this book:

16

Paperback ○   Hardback ○   e-book ○   Audiobook ○

Title:

Dates
Started: _____
Finished: _____

Source
Bought ○   Loaned ○
From: _____

Author: _____
Publisher: _____   Pub. date _____
Page count: _____
○ Fiction   ○ Non-fiction
  Genre: _____   Subject: _____

My Review:

Inspiration Tree

Why I read it?
_____

It inspired me to
(read/learn/visit)?
_____
_____

Who will I
recommend it to?
_____

＊ Ratings ＊

Plot: 1 2 3 4 5
Characters:
1 2 3 4 5
Ease of reading:
1 2 3 4 5
Overall
☹ 😐 ☺

Great quotes from this book:

Paperback ○   Hardback ○   e-book ○   Audiobook ○

17

Title:

Author: _____

Publisher: _____ Pub. date _____

Page count: _____

○ Fiction   ○ Non-fiction

Genre: _____   Subject: _____

Dates
Started: _____
Finished: _____

Source
Bought ○   Loaned ○
From: _____

My Review: _____

_____

_____

_____

_____

_____

_____

_____

_____

_____

_____

_____

_____

_____

_____

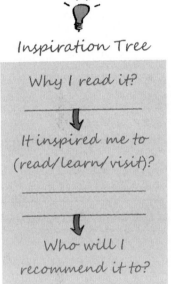

Inspiration Tree

Why I read it?
_____
↓
It inspired me to
(read/learn/visit)?
_____
_____
↓
Who will I
recommend it to?
_____

✳ Ratings ✳

Plot: 1 2 3 4 5
Characters:
1 2 3 4 5
Ease of reading:
1 2 3 4 5
Overall
😞 😐 😊

Great quotes from this book:

18

Paperback ○   Hardback ○   e-book ○   Audiobook ○

Title:

Dates
Started: _____
Finished: _____

Source
Bought ○   Loaned ○
From: _____

Author: _____
Publisher: _____   Pub. date _____
Page count: _____
○ Fiction   ○ Non-fiction
  Genre: _____   Subject: _____

My Review:

_____
_____
_____
_____
_____
_____
_____
_____
_____
_____
_____
_____
_____

Inspiration Tree

Why I read it?
_____
↓
It inspired me to
(read/learn/visit)?
_____
↓
Who will I
recommend it to?
_____

✳ Ratings ✳

Plot: 1 2 3 4 5
Characters:
1 2 3 4 5
Ease of reading:
1 2 3 4 5
Overall
☹ 😐 🙂

Great quotes from this book:

Paperback ○   Hardback ○   e-book ○   Audiobook ○

19

Title:

Author:

Publisher: _____ Pub. date _____

Page count: _____

○ Fiction   ○ Non-fiction
  Genre: _____   Subject: _____

Dates
Started: _____
Finished: _____

Source
Bought ○ Loaned ○
From: _____

My Review: _____

_____

_____

_____

_____

_____

_____

_____

_____

_____

_____

_____

_____

_____

_____

_____

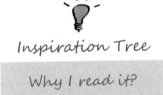

Inspiration Tree

Why I read it?
_____
↓
It inspired me to
(read/learn/visit)?
_____
_____
↓
Who will I
recommend it to?
_____

✳ Ratings ✳

Plot: 1 2 3 4 5
Characters:
1 2 3 4 5
Ease of reading:
1 2 3 4 5
Overall
☹ 😐 🙂

Great quotes from this book:

20

Title:

Dates
Started: _____
Finished: _____

Source
Bought ○   Loaned ○
From: _____

Author: _____
Publisher: _____   Pub. date _____
Page count: _____
○ Fiction   ○ Non-fiction
  Genre: _____   Subject: _____

My Review:
_____
_____
_____
_____
_____
_____
_____
_____
_____
_____
_____
_____
_____
_____

Inspiration Tree

Why I read it?
_____
↓
It inspired me to
(read/learn/visit)?
_____
_____
↓
Who will I
recommend it to?
_____

✶ Ratings ✶

Plot: 1 2 3 4 5
Characters:
1 2 3 4 5
Ease of reading:
1 2 3 4 5
Overall
☹ 😐 ☺

Great quotes from this book:

Paperback ○   Hardback ○   e-book ○   Audiobook ○

21

Title:

Author: _____

Publisher: _____ Pub. date _____

Page count: _____

○ Fiction   ○ Non-fiction
Genre: _____   Subject: _____

Dates
Started: _____
Finished: _____

Source
Bought ○   Loaned ○
From: _____

My Review: _____
_____
_____
_____
_____
_____
_____
_____
_____
_____
_____
_____
_____
_____

Inspiration Tree

Why I read it?
_____
↓
It inspired me to
(read/learn/visit)?
_____
_____
↓
Who will I
recommend it to?
_____

✳ Ratings ✳

Plot: 1 2 3 4 5
Characters:
1 2 3 4 5
Ease of reading:
1 2 3 4 5

Overall

Great quotes from this book:

22

Title:

Dates

Started: _____

Finished: _____

Source

Bought ○   Loaned ○

From: _____

Author: _____

Publisher: _____   Pub. date _____

Page count: _____

○ Fiction   ○ Non-fiction

Genre: _____   Subject: _____

Inspiration Tree

Why I read it?

_____

⬇

It inspired me to (read/learn/visit)?

_____

⬇

Who will I recommend it to?

_____

✳ Ratings ✳

Plot: 1   2   3   4   5

Characters:

1   2   3   4   5

Ease of reading:

1   2   3   4   5

Overall

☹   😐   ☺

My Review:

_____
_____
_____
_____
_____
_____
_____
_____
_____
_____
_____
_____

Great quotes from this book:

Paperback ○   Hardback ○   e-book ○   Audiobook ○

23

Title:

Author: _____

Publisher: _____ Pub. date _____

Page count: _____

○ Fiction   ○ Non-fiction

  Genre: _____   Subject: _____

Dates
Started: _____
Finished: _____

Source
Bought ○ Loaned ○
From: _____

My Review: _____

_____

_____

_____

_____

_____

_____

_____

_____

_____

_____

_____

_____

_____

_____

Great quotes from this book:

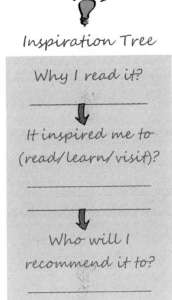

Inspiration Tree

Why I read it?
_____
↓
It inspired me to
(read/learn/visit)?
_____
_____
↓
Who will I
recommend it to?
_____

※ Ratings ※

Plot: 1 2 3 4 5
Characters:
1 2 3 4 5
Ease of reading:
1 2 3 4 5
Overall
☹ 😐 🙂

24

Title:

Dates
Started: _____
Finished: _____

Source
Bought ○　Loaned ○
From: _____

Author: _____
Publisher: _____　　　Pub. date _____
Page count: _____
○ Fiction　　　　　　　　　○ Non-fiction
　Genre: _____　　　　Subject: _____

My Review: _____

Inspiration Tree

Why I read it?
_____
↓
It inspired me to
(read/learn/visit)?
_____
_____
↓
Who will I
recommend it to?
_____

＊ Ratings ＊

Plot: 1 2 3 4 5
Characters:
1 2 3 4 5
Ease of reading:
1 2 3 4 5
Overall
☹ 😐 🙂

Great quotes from this book:

Paperback ○   Hardback ○   e-book ○   Audiobook ○

25

Title:

Author: _____

Publisher: _____   Pub. date _____

Page count: _____

○ Fiction   ○ Non-fiction

   Genre: _____   Subject: _____

Dates
Started: _____
Finished: _____

Source
Bought ○ Loaned ○
From: _____

My Review: _____
_____
_____
_____
_____
_____
_____
_____
_____
_____
_____
_____
_____
_____
_____

Inspiration Tree

Why I read it?
_____

It inspired me to
(read/learn/visit)?
_____
_____

Who will I
recommend it to?
_____

✳ Ratings ✳

Plot: 1 2 3 4 5
Characters:
1 2 3 4 5
Ease of reading:
1 2 3 4 5
Overall
☹ 😐 ☺

Great quotes from this book:

26

Title:

Dates
Started: _____
Finished: _____

Source
Bought ○   Loaned ○
From: _____

Inspiration Tree

Why I read it?
_____
↓
It inspired me to
(read/learn/visit)?
_____
_____
↓
Who will I
recommend it to?
_____

✳ Ratings ✳

Plot: 1 2 3 4 5
Characters:
1 2 3 4 5
Ease of reading:
1 2 3 4 5
Overall

Author: _____
Publisher: _____   Pub. date _____
Page count: _____
○ Fiction   ○ Non-fiction
   Genre: _____   Subject: _____

My Review: _____
_____
_____
_____
_____
_____
_____
_____
_____
_____
_____
_____
_____
_____

Great quotes from this book:

Paperback ○   Hardback ○   e-book ○   Audiobook ○

27

Title:

Author: _____

Publisher: _____ Pub. date _____

Page count: _____

○ Fiction   ○ Non-fiction

  Genre: _____   Subject: _____

Dates
Started: _____
Finished: _____

Source
Bought ○ Loaned ○
From: _____

My Review: _____

_____

_____

_____

_____

_____

_____

_____

_____

_____

_____

_____

_____

_____

_____

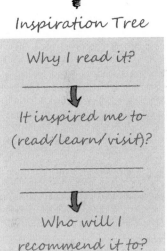

Inspiration Tree

Why I read it?
_____

It inspired me to
(read/learn/visit)?
_____
_____

Who will I
recommend it to?
_____

✳ Ratings ✳

Plot: 1 2 3 4 5
Characters:
1 2 3 4 5
Ease of reading:
1 2 3 4 5
Overall
☹ 😐 ☺

Great quotes from this book:

28

Title:

Dates

Started: _____

Finished: _____

Source

Bought ○   Loaned ○

From: _____

Author: _____

Publisher: _____   Pub. date _____

Page count: _____

○ Fiction   ○ Non-fiction

Genre: _____   Subject: _____

My Review:

_____

_____

_____

_____

_____

_____

_____

_____

_____

_____

_____

_____

Inspiration Tree

Why I read it?

_____

↓

It inspired me to (read/learn/visit)?

_____

↓

Who will I recommend it to?

_____

✳ Ratings ✳

Plot: 1 2 3 4 5

Characters:
1 2 3 4 5

Ease of reading:
1 2 3 4 5

Overall

☹ 😐 🙂

Great quotes from this book:

Paperback ○   Hardback ○   e-book ○   Audiobook ○

29

Title:

Author: _____

Publisher: _____   Pub. date _____

Page count: _____

○ Fiction   ○ Non-fiction
  Genre: _____   Subject: _____

Dates
Started: _____
Finished: _____

Source
Bought ○   Loaned ○
From: _____

My Review: -
_____
_____
_____
_____
_____
_____
_____
_____
_____
_____
_____
_____
_____
_____
_____
_____
_____
_____

Inspiration Tree

Why I read it?
_____
↓
It inspired me to
(read/learn/visit)?
_____
↓
Who will I
recommend it to?
_____

✳ Ratings ✳

Plot: 1 2 3 4 5
Characters:
1 2 3 4 5
Ease of reading:
1 2 3 4 5
Overall
☹ 😐 ☺

Great quotes from this book:

30

Title: _____

Dates
Started: _____
Finished: _____

Source
Bought ○   Loaned ○
From: _____

Author: _____
Publisher: _____   Pub. date _____
Page count: _____
○ Fiction   ○ Non-fiction
   Genre: _____   Subject: _____

My Review:

_____
_____
_____
_____
_____
_____
_____
_____
_____
_____
_____
_____
_____
_____
_____
_____

Inspiration Tree

Why I read it?
_____
↓
It inspired me to
(read/learn/visit)?
_____
_____
↓
Who will I
recommend it to?
_____

✳ Ratings ✳

Plot: 1 2 3 4 5
Characters:
1 2 3 4 5
Ease of reading:
1 2 3 4 5
Overall
☹ 😐 ☺

Great quotes from this book:

Paperback ○   Hardback ○   e-book ○   Audiobook ○

31

Title:

Author: _____

Publisher: _____ Pub. date _____

Page count: _____

○ Fiction   ○ Non-fiction

  Genre: _____   Subject: _____

Dates
Started: _____
Finished: _____

Source
Bought ○ Loaned ○
From: _____

My Review: _____
_____
_____
_____
_____
_____
_____
_____
_____
_____
_____
_____
_____
_____
_____
_____
_____
_____
_____
_____
_____

Great quotes from this book:

Inspiration Tree

Why I read it?
_____

It inspired me to
(read/learn/visit)?
_____
_____

Who will I
recommend it to?
_____

✳ Ratings ✳

Plot: 1 2 3 4 5

Characters:
1 2 3 4 5

Ease of reading:
1 2 3 4 5

Overall
☹ 😐 ☺

32

Title:

Dates
Started: _____
Finished: _____

Source
Bought ○ Loaned ○
From: _____

Author: _____
Publisher: _____   Pub. date _____
Page count: _____
○ Fiction   ○ Non-fiction
   Genre: _____   Subject: _____

My Review:
_____
_____
_____
_____
_____
_____
_____
_____
_____
_____
_____
_____
_____
_____
_____
_____

Inspiration Tree

Why I read it?
_____
⬇
It inspired me to
(read/learn/visit)?
_____
_____
⬇
Who will I
recommend it to?
_____

✳ Ratings ✳

Plot: 1 2 3 4 5
Characters:
1 2 3 4 5
Ease of reading:
1 2 3 4 5
Overall
☹ 😐 ☺

Great quotes from this book:

Paperback ○   Hardback ○   e-book ○   Audiobook ○

33

Title:

Author: _____

Publisher: _____ Pub. date _____

Page count: _____

○ Fiction   ○ Non-fiction

Genre: _____   Subject: _____

Dates
Started: _____
Finished: _____

Source
Bought ○ Loaned ○
From: _____

My Review: _____

_____

_____

_____

_____

_____

_____

_____

_____

_____

_____

_____

Great quotes from this book:

Inspiration Tree

Why I read it?

_____
↓

It inspired me to
(read/learn/visit)?

_____
↓

Who will I
recommend it to?

_____

✳ Ratings ✳

Plot: 1 2 3 4 5

Characters:
1 2 3 4 5

Ease of reading:
1 2 3 4 5

Overall

☹ 😐 😊

34

Title:

Dates
Started: _____
Finished: _____

Source
Bought ○   Loaned ○
From: _____

Author: _____
Publisher: _____   Pub. date _____
Page count: _____
○ Fiction   ○ Non-fiction
   Genre: _____   Subject: _____

My Review:

_____
_____
_____
_____
_____
_____
_____
_____
_____
_____
_____
_____

Inspiration Tree

Why I read it?
_____
↓
It inspired me to
(read/learn/visit)?
_____
_____
↓
Who will I
recommend it to?
_____

✳ Ratings ✳

Plot: 1 2 3 4 5
Characters:
1 2 3 4 5
Ease of reading:
1 2 3 4 5
Overall
☹ 😐 ☺

Great quotes from this book:

Paperback ○   Hardback ○   e-book ○   Audiobook ○

35

Title:

Author: _____

Publisher: _____   Pub. date _____

Page count: _____

○ Fiction   ○ Non-fiction

Genre: _____   Subject: _____

Dates
Started: _____
Finished: _____

Source
Bought ○   Loaned ○
From: _____

My Review: _____

_____

_____

_____

_____

_____

_____

_____

_____

_____

_____

_____

_____

_____

_____

_____

_____

Great quotes from this book:

Inspiration Tree

Why I read it?
_____

It inspired me to
(read/learn/visit)?
_____
_____

Who will I
recommend it to?
_____

✳ Ratings ✳

Plot: 1 2 3 4 5
Characters:
1 2 3 4 5
Ease of reading:
1 2 3 4 5
Overall
☹ 😐 ☺

36

Paperback ○   Hardback ○   e-book ○   Audiobook ○

Title:

Dates
Started: _____
Finished: _____

Source
Bought ○ Loaned ○
From: _____

💡

Inspiration Tree

Why I read it?
_____
⬇
It inspired me to
(read/learn/visit)?
_____
⬇
Who will I
recommend it to?
_____

✳ Ratings ✳

Plot: 1 2 3 4 5
Characters:
1 2 3 4 5
Ease of reading:
1 2 3 4 5
Overall
☹ 😐 🙂

Author: _____
Publisher: _____   Pub. date _____
Page count: _____
○ Fiction   ○ Non-fiction
  Genre: _____   Subject: _____

My Review: _____
_____
_____
_____
_____
_____
_____
_____
_____
_____
_____
_____

Great quotes from this book:

Paperback ○   Hardback ○   e-book ○   Audiobook ○

37

Title:

Author: _____

Publisher: _____   Pub. date _____

Page count: _____

○ Fiction   ○ Non-fiction
  Genre: _____   Subject: _____

Dates
Started: _____
Finished: _____

Source
Bought ○   Loaned ○
From: _____

My Review: _____
_____
_____
_____
_____
_____
_____
_____
_____
_____
_____
_____
_____
_____
_____
_____

Inspiration Tree

Why I read it?
_____
⬇
It inspired me to
(read/learn/visit)?
_____
_____
⬇
Who will I
recommend it to?
_____

✳ Ratings ✳

Plot: 1 2 3 4 5
Characters:
1 2 3 4 5
Ease of reading:
1 2 3 4 5
Overall
☹ 😐 🙂

Great quotes from this book:

38

Title:

Dates
Started: _____
Finished: _____

Source
Bought O Loaned O
From: _____

Inspiration Tree

Why I read it?
_____
↓
It inspired me to
(read/learn/visit)?
_____
_____
↓
Who will I
recommend it to?
_____

✳ Ratings ✳

Plot: 1 2 3 4 5
Characters:
1 2 3 4 5
Ease of reading:
1 2 3 4 5
Overall
☹ 😐 ☺

Author: _____
Publisher: _____ Pub. date _____
Page count: _____
O Fiction   O Non-fiction
  Genre: _____   Subject: _____

My Review: _____
_____
_____
_____
_____
_____
_____
_____
_____
_____
_____
_____
_____

Great quotes from this book:

Paperback ○   Hardback ○   e-book ○   Audiobook ○

39

Title:

Author: _____

Publisher: _____   Pub. date _____

Page count: _____

○ Fiction   ○ Non-fiction

Genre: _____   Subject: _____

Dates
Started: _____
Finished: _____

Source
Bought ○ Loaned ○

From: _____

My Review: _____
_____
_____
_____
_____
_____
_____
_____
_____
_____
_____
_____
_____

Inspiration Tree

Why I read it?
_____
↓
It inspired me to
(read/learn/visit)?
_____
_____
↓
Who will I
recommend it to?
_____

✳ Ratings ✳

Plot: 1 2 3 4 5
Characters:
1 2 3 4 5
Ease of reading:
1 2 3 4 5
Overall
☹ 😐 😊

Great quotes from this book:

Paperback ○   Hardback ○   e-book ○   Audiobook ○

Title:

Dates
Started: _____
Finished: _____

Source
Bought ○ Loaned ○
From: _____

Author: _____
Publisher: _____   Pub. date _____
Page count: _____
○ Fiction   ○ Non-fiction
  Genre: _____   Subject: _____

My Review:

_____
_____
_____
_____
_____
_____
_____
_____
_____
_____
_____
_____
_____
_____
_____

Inspiration Tree

Why I read it?
_____

It inspired me to
(read/learn/visit)?
_____

Who will I
recommend it to?
_____

✳ Ratings ✳

Plot: 1 2 3 4 5
Characters:
1 2 3 4 5
Ease of reading:
1 2 3 4 5
Overall
☹ 😐 ☺

Great quotes from this book:

Paperback ○   Hardback ○   e-book ○   Audiobook ○

41

Title:

Author: _____

Publisher: _____   Pub. date _____

Page count: _____

○ Fiction   ○ Non-fiction

Genre: _____   Subject: _____

Dates
Started: _____
Finished: _____

Source
Bought ○ Loaned ○
From: _____

My Review: _____

_____

_____

_____

_____

_____

_____

_____

_____

_____

_____

_____

Inspiration Tree

Why I read it?
_____
↓
It inspired me to
(read/learn/visit)?
_____
_____
↓
Who will I
recommend it to?
_____

✵ Ratings ✵

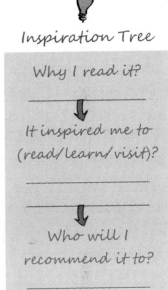

Plot: 1 2 3 4 5
Characters:
1 2 3 4 5
Ease of reading:
1 2 3 4 5
Overall
☹ 😐 ☺

Great quotes from this book:

42

Title:

Dates
Started: _____
Finished: _____

Source
Bought ○   Loaned ○
From: _____

Author: _____
Publisher: _____   Pub. date _____
Page count: _____
○ Fiction   ○ Non-fiction
   Genre: _____   Subject: _____

My Review: _____
_____
_____
_____
_____
_____
_____
_____
_____
_____
_____
_____
_____
_____

💡
Inspiration Tree

Why I read it?
_____
⬇
It inspired me to
(read/learn/visit)?
_____
⬇
Who will I
recommend it to?
_____

✳ Ratings ✳

Plot: 1 2 3 4 5
Characters:
1 2 3 4 5
Ease of reading:
1 2 3 4 5
Overall
☹ 😐 🙂

Great quotes from this book:

Paperback ○   Hardback ○   e-book ○   Audiobook ○

43

Title:

Author: _____

Publisher: _____   Pub. date _____

Page count: _____

○ Fiction   ○ Non-fiction

  Genre: _____   Subject: _____

Dates
Started: _____
Finished: _____

Source
Bought ○ Loaned ○
From: _____

My Review: _____

_____

_____

_____

_____

_____

_____

_____

_____

_____

_____

_____

Inspiration Tree

Why I read it?
_____
↓
It inspired me to
(read/learn/visit)?
_____
_____
↓
Who will I
recommend it to?
_____

✳ Ratings ✳

Plot: 1 2 3 4 5
Characters:
1 2 3 4 5
Ease of reading:
1 2 3 4 5
Overall
☹ 😐 ☺

Great quotes from this book:

Paperback O   Hardback O   e-book O   Audiobook O

Title:

Author: _____

Publisher: _____   Pub. date _____

Page count: _____

O Fiction   O Non-fiction

  Genre: _____   Subject: _____

Dates

Started: _____

Finished: _____

Source

Bought O   Loaned O

From: _____

Inspiration Tree

Why I read it?

_____

⬇

It inspired me to
(read/learn/visit)?

_____

_____

⬇

Who will I
recommend it to?

_____

✳ Ratings ✳

Plot: 1 2 3 4 5

Characters:
1 2 3 4 5

Ease of reading:
1 2 3 4 5

Overall

☹ 😐 🙂

My Review: _____

_____

_____

_____

_____

_____

_____

_____

_____

_____

_____

_____

_____

Great quotes from this book:

Paperback ○   Hardback ○   e-book ○   Audiobook ○

45

Title:

Author: _____

Publisher: _____   Pub. date _____

Page count: _____

○ Fiction   ○ Non-fiction

  Genre: _____   Subject: _____

Dates
Started: _____
Finished: _____

Source
Bought ○ Loaned ○
From: _____

My Review: _____

_____

_____

_____

_____

_____

_____

_____

_____

_____

_____

_____

_____

_____

Great quotes from this book:

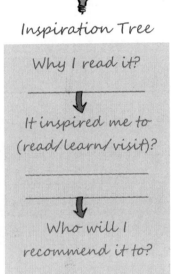

Inspiration Tree

Why I read it?
_____
↓
It inspired me to
(read/learn/visit)?
_____
_____
↓
Who will I
recommend it to?
_____

✳ Ratings ✳

Plot: 1 2 3 4 5
Characters:
1 2 3 4 5
Ease of reading:
1 2 3 4 5
Overall
☹ 😐 🙂

46

Title:

Dates
Started: _____
Finished: _____

Source
Bought ○ Loaned ○
From: _____

Author: _____
Publisher: _____   Pub. date _____
Page count: _____
○ Fiction   ○ Non-fiction
  Genre: _____   Subject: _____

My Review: _____

Inspiration Tree

Why I read it?
_____
↓
It inspired me to
(read/learn/visit)?
_____
↓
Who will I
recommend it to?
_____

_____
_____
_____
_____
_____
_____
_____
_____
_____
_____
_____
_____
_____

✳ Ratings ✳

Plot: 1 2 3 4 5
Characters:
1 2 3 4 5
Ease of reading:
1 2 3 4 5
Overall
☹ 😐 🙂

Great quotes from this book:

Paperback ○   Hardback ○   e-book ○   Audiobook ○

47

Title:

Author: _____

Publisher: _____ Pub. date _____

Page count: _____

○ Fiction   ○ Non-fiction

Genre: _____   Subject: _____

Dates
Started: _____
Finished: _____

Source
Bought ○ Loaned ○
From: _____

My Review: _____
_____
_____
_____
_____
_____
_____
_____
_____
_____
_____
_____
_____
_____
_____

Great quotes from this book:

Inspiration Tree

Why I read it?
_____
↓
It inspired me to
(read/learn/visit)?
_____
_____
↓
Who will I
recommend it to?
_____

✳ Ratings ✳

Plot: 1 2 3 4 5
Characters:
1 2 3 4 5
Ease of reading:
1 2 3 4 5
Overall
☹ 😐 😊

48

Title:

Dates
Started: _____
Finished: _____

Source
Bought ○   Loaned ○
From: _____

Author: _____
Publisher: _____   Pub. date _____
Page count: _____
○ Fiction   ○ Non-fiction
  Genre: _____   Subject: _____

My Review:

_____
_____
_____
_____
_____
_____
_____
_____
_____
_____
_____
_____
_____
_____

Inspiration Tree

Why I read it?
_____
↓
It inspired me to
(read/learn/visit)?
_____
_____
↓
Who will I
recommend it to?
_____

✳ Ratings ✳

Plot: 1 2 3 4 5
Characters:
1 2 3 4 5
Ease of reading:
1 2 3 4 5
Overall
☹ 😐 🙂

Great quotes from this book:

Paperback ○   Hardback ○   e-book ○   Audiobook ○

49

Title:

Author: _____

Publisher: _____   Pub. date _____

Page count: _____

○ Fiction   ○ Non-fiction

  Genre: _____   Subject: _____

Dates
Started: _____
Finished: _____

Source
Bought ○   Loaned ○
From: _____

My Review: _____
_____
_____
_____
_____
_____
_____
_____
_____
_____
_____
_____
_____

Inspiration Tree

Why I read it?
_____
⬇
It inspired me to
(read/learn/visit)?
_____
_____
⬇
Who will I
recommend it to?
_____

Great quotes from this book:

✳ Ratings ✳

Plot: 1 2 3 4 5
Characters:
1 2 3 4 5
Ease of reading:
1 2 3 4 5
Overall
☹ 😐 🙂

50

Paperback ○   Hardback ○   e-book ○   Audiobook ○

Title:

Dates
Started: _____
Finished: _____

Source
Bought ○   Loaned ○
From: _____

Author: _____
Publisher: _____   Pub. date _____
Page count: _____
○ Fiction   ○ Non-fiction
   Genre: _____   Subject: _____

My Review:

_____
_____
_____
_____
_____
_____
_____
_____
_____
_____
_____
_____
_____
_____

💡

Inspiration Tree

Why I read it?
_____
⬇
It inspired me to
(read/learn/visit)?
_____
⬇
Who will I
recommend it to?
_____

✴ Ratings ✴

Plot: 1 2 3 4 5
Characters:
1 2 3 4 5
Ease of reading:
1 2 3 4 5
Overall
☹ 😐 🙂

Great quotes from this book:

Paperback ○   Hardback ○   e-book ○   Audiobook ○

51

Title:

Author: _____

Publisher: _____   Pub. date _____

Page count: _____

○ Fiction   ○ Non-fiction

Genre: _____   Subject: _____

Dates
Started: _____
Finished: _____

Source
Bought ○ Loaned ○
From: _____

My Review: ....

_____
_____
_____
_____
_____
_____
_____
_____
_____
_____
_____
_____
_____
_____
_____
_____
_____

Inspiration Tree

Why I read it?

_____
↓
It inspired me to
(read/learn/visit)?

_____
↓
Who will I
recommend it to?

_____

✳ Ratings ✳

Plot: 1 2 3 4 5

Characters:
1 2 3 4 5

Ease of reading:
1 2 3 4 5

Overall
☹ 😐 ☺

Great quotes from this book:

52

Paperback ○   Hardback ○   e-book ○   Audiobook ○

Title:

Author: _____

Publisher: _____   Pub. date _____

Page count: _____

○ Fiction   ○ Non-fiction

  Genre: _____   Subject: _____

Dates
Started: _____
Finished: _____

Source
Bought ○ Loaned ○
From: _____

Inspiration Tree

Why I read it?
_____
↓
It inspired me to
(read/learn/visit)?
_____
↓
Who will I
recommend it to?
_____

✳ Ratings ✳

Plot: 1 2 3 4 5
Characters:
1 2 3 4 5
Ease of reading:
1 2 3 4 5
Overall
☹ 😐 ☺

My Review:

_____
_____
_____
_____
_____
_____
_____
_____
_____
_____
_____
_____
_____

Great quotes from this book:

Paperback ○   Hardback ○   e-book ○   Audiobook ○

53

Title:

Author:

Publisher: Pub. date

Page count:

○ Fiction   ○ Non-fiction
  Genre: Subject.

Dates
Started: _____
Finished: _____

Source
Bought ○   Loaned ○
From: _____

My Review:

Inspiration Tree

Why I read it?

⬇

It inspired me to
(read/learn/visit)?

⬇

Who will I
recommend it to?

✳ Ratings ✳

Plot: 1 2 3 4 5
Characters.
1 2 3 4 5
Ease of reading:
1 2 3 4 5

Overall
☹ 😐 ☺

Great quotes from this book:

54

Paperback ○   Hardback ○   e-book ○   Audiobook ○

Title:

Dates
Started: _____
Finished: _____

Source
Bought ○   Loaned ○
From: _____

Inspiration Tree

Why I read it?
_____
↓
It inspired me to
(read/learn/visit)?
_____
_____
↓
Who will I
recommend it to?
_____

✳ Ratings ✳

Plot: 1 2 3 4 5
Characters:
1 2 3 4 5
Ease of reading:
1 2 3 4 5
Overall
☹ 😐 🙂

Author: _____
Publisher: _____   Pub. date _____
Page count: _____
○ Fiction   ○ Non-fiction
   Genre: _____   Subject: _____

My Review:
_____
_____
_____
_____
_____
_____
_____
_____
_____
_____
_____
_____
_____

Great quotes from this book:

Paperback ○   Hardback ○   e-book ○   Audiobook ○

55

Title:

Author: _____

Publisher: _____   Pub. date _____

Page count: _____

○ Fiction   ○ Non-fiction
  Genre: _____   Subject: _____

Dates
Started: _____
Finished: _____

Source
Bought ○ Loaned ○
From: _____

My Review: _____
_____
_____
_____
_____
_____
_____
_____
_____
_____
_____
_____
_____

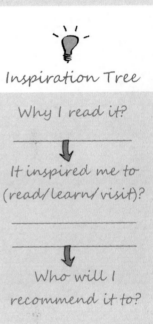

Inspiration Tree

Why I read it?
_____
↓
It inspired me to
(read/learn/visit)?
_____
_____
↓
Who will I
recommend it to?
_____

✳ Ratings ✳

Plot: 1 2 3 4 5
Characters:
1 2 3 4 5
Ease of reading:
1 2 3 4 5
Overall
☹ 😐 🙂

Great quotes from this book:

56

Title:

Dates
Started: _____
Finished: _____

Source
Bought ○ Loaned ○
From: _____

Author: _____
Publisher: _____ Pub. date _____
Page count: _____
○ Fiction   ○ Non-fiction
  Genre: _____   Subject: _____

My Review:
_____
_____
_____
_____
_____
_____
_____
_____
_____
_____
_____
_____
_____
_____
_____

Inspiration Tree

Why I read it?
_____

It inspired me to
(read/learn/visit)?
_____
_____

Who will I
recommend it to?
_____

✳ Ratings ✳

Plot: 1 2 3 4 5
Characters:
1 2 3 4 5
Ease of reading:
1 2 3 4 5
Overall
☹ 😐 😊

Great quotes from this book:

Paperback ○   Hardback ○   e-book ○   Audiobook ○

Title:

Author: _____

Publisher: _____ Pub. date _____

Page count: _____

○ Fiction   ○ Non-fiction

  Genre: _____   Subject: _____

Dates
Started: _____
Finished: _____

Source
Bought ○ Loaned ○
From: _____

My Review: _____
_____
_____
_____
_____
_____
_____
_____
_____
_____
_____
_____

Inspiration Tree

Why I read it?
_____
↓
It inspired me to
(read/learn/visit)?
_____
_____
↓
Who will I
recommend it to?
_____

Great quotes from this book:

✳ Ratings ✳

Plot: 1 2 3 4 5

Characters:
1 2 3 4 5

Ease of reading:
1 2 3 4 5

Overall

58

Paperback ○   Hardback ○   e-book ○   Audiobook ○

Title:

Dates

Started: _____

Finished: _____

Source

Bought ○   Loaned ○

From: _____

Author: _____

Publisher: _____   Pub. date _____

Page count: _____

○ Fiction   ○ Non-fiction

   Genre: _____   Subject: _____

Inspiration Tree

Why I read it?

_____

↓

It inspired me to
(read/learn/visit)?

_____

↓

Who will I
recommend it to?

_____

My Review: _____

_____

_____

_____

_____

_____

_____

_____

_____

_____

_____

_____

_____

_____

_____

_____

_____

✳ Ratings ✳

Plot: 1   2   3   4   5

Characters:

1   2   3   4   5

Ease of reading:

1   2   3   4   5

Overall

☹   😐   🙂

Great quotes from this book:

Paperback ○   Hardback ○   e-book ○   Audiobook ○

59

Title:

Author: _____

Publisher: _____   Pub. date _____

Page count: _____

○ Fiction   ○ Non-fiction

Genre: _____   Subject: _____

Dates
Started: _____
Finished: _____

Source
Bought ○   Loaned ○
From: _____

My Review: _____

_____

_____

_____

_____

_____

_____

_____

_____

_____

_____

_____

_____

Inspiration Tree

Why I read it?
_____
↓
It inspired me to
(read/learn/visit)?
_____
↓
Who will I
recommend it to?
_____

⁂ Ratings ⁂

Plot: 1 2 3 4 5
Characters:
1 2 3 4 5
Ease of reading:
1 2 3 4 5
Overall
☹ 😐 ☺

Great quotes from this book:

60

Title:

Dates
Started: _____
Finished: _____

Source
Bought ○ Loaned ○
From: _____

Author: _____
Publisher: _____ Pub. date _____
Page count: _____
○ Fiction   ○ Non-fiction
   Genre: _____   Subject: _____

My Review:
_____
_____
_____
_____
_____
_____
_____
_____
_____
_____
_____
_____

💡
Inspiration Tree

Why I read it?
_____
⬇
It inspired me to
(read/learn/visit)?
_____
⬇
Who will I
recommend it to?
_____

✳ Ratings ✳

Plot: 1 2 3 4 5
Characters:
1 2 3 4 5
Ease of reading:
1 2 3 4 5
Overall
☹ 😐 ☺

Great quotes from this book:

Paperback ○   Hardback ○   e-book ○   Audiobook ○

61

Title:

Author:

Publisher: _____ Pub. date _____

Page count: _____

○ Fiction   ○ Non-fiction

Genre: _____   Subject: _____

Dates
Started: _____
Finished: _____

Source
Bought ○   Loaned ○
From: _____

My Review: _____

_____

_____

_____

_____

_____

_____

_____

_____

_____

_____

_____

_____

_____

Inspiration Tree

Why I read it?
_____
↓
It inspired me to
(read/learn/visit)?
_____
_____
↓
Who will I
recommend it to?
_____

✳ Ratings ✳

Plot: 1 2 3 4 5
Characters:
1 2 3 4 5
Ease of reading:
1 2 3 4 5
Overall
☹ 😐 ☺

Great quotes from this book:

62

Title:

Dates
Started: _____
Finished: _____

Source
Bought ○   Loaned ○
From: _____

Author: _____
Publisher: _____   Pub. date _____
Page count: _____
○ Fiction
   Genre: _____

○ Non-fiction
   Subject: _____

My Review:

_____
_____
_____
_____
_____
_____
_____
_____
_____
_____
_____
_____
_____

Inspiration Tree

Why I read it?
_____
↓
It inspired me to
(read/learn/visit)?
_____
↓
Who will I
recommend it to?
_____

✳ Ratings ✳

Plot: 1 2 3 4 5
Characters:
1 2 3 4 5
Ease of reading:
1 2 3 4 5
Overall
☹ 😐 😊

Great quotes from this book:

Paperback ○   Hardback ○   e-book ○   Audiobook ○

63

Title:

Author: _____

Publisher: _____   Pub. date _____

Page count: _____

○ Fiction   ○ Non-fiction
   Genre: _____   Subject: _____

Dates
Started: _____
Finished: _____

Source
Bought ○   Loaned ○
From: _____

My Review: _____
_____
_____
_____
_____
_____
_____
_____
_____
_____
_____
_____
_____
_____

Great quotes from this book:

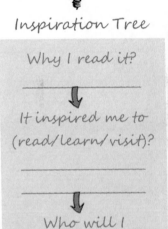

Inspiration Tree

Why I read it?
_____
↓
It inspired me to
(read/learn/visit)?
_____
_____
↓
Who will I
recommend it to?
_____

✳ Ratings ✳

Plot: 1 2 3 4 5
Characters:
1 2 3 4 5
Ease of reading:
1 2 3 4 5
Overall
☹ 😐 ☺

Paperback ○   Hardback ○   e-book ○   Audiobook ○

Title:

Dates
Started: _____
Finished: _____

Source
Bought ○ Loaned ○
From: _____

Author: _____
Publisher: _____ Pub. date _____
Page count: _____
○ Fiction   ○ Non-fiction
  Genre: _____   Subject: _____

My Review:

_____
_____
_____
_____
_____
_____
_____
_____
_____
_____
_____
_____
_____
_____

Inspiration Tree

Why I read it?
_____
↓
It inspired me to
(read/learn/visit)?
_____
_____
↓
Who will I
recommend it to?
_____

✳ Ratings ✳

Plot: 1 2 3 4 5
Characters:
1 2 3 4 5
Ease of reading:
1 2 3 4 5
Overall
☹ 😐 ☺

Great quotes from this book:

Paperback ○   Hardback ○   e-book ○   Audiobook ○

65

Title:

Author: _____

Publisher: _____   Pub. date _____

Page count: _____

○ Fiction   ○ Non-fiction

Genre: _____   Subject: _____

Dates
Started: _____
Finished: _____

Source
Bought ○   Loaned ○
From: _____

My Review: _____
_____
_____
_____
_____
_____
_____
_____
_____
_____
_____
_____
_____

Great quotes from this book:

Inspiration Tree

Why I read it?
_____
↓
It inspired me to
(read/learn/visit)?
_____
↓
Who will I
recommend it to?
_____

✳ Ratings ✳

Plot: 1 2 3 4 5
Characters:
1 2 3 4 5
Ease of reading:
1 2 3 4 5
Overall

66

Paperback ○　　Hardback ○　　e-book ○　　Audiobook ○

Title:

Dates
Started: _____
Finished: _____

Source
Bought ○　Loaned ○
From: _____

Inspiration Tree

Why I read it?
_____
↓
It inspired me to
(read/learn/visit)?
_____
↓
Who will I
recommend it to?
_____

✳ Ratings ✳

Plot: 1 2 3 4 5
Characters:
1 2 3 4 5
Ease of reading:
1 2 3 4 5
Overall
☹ 😐 ☺

Author: _____
Publisher: _____　　Pub. date _____
Page count: _____
○ Fiction　　　　　　　　　　○ Non-fiction
　Genre: _____　　　　Subject: _____

My Review:
_____
_____
_____
_____
_____
_____
_____
_____
_____
_____
_____
_____
_____
_____

Great quotes from this book:

Paperback ○   Hardback ○   e-book ○   Audiobook ○

Title:

Author: _____

Publisher: _____   Pub. date _____

Page count: _____

○ Fiction   ○ Non-fiction
  Genre: _____   Subject: _____

Dates
Started: _____
Finished: _____

Source
Bought ○ Loaned ○
From: _____

My Review: _____
_____
_____
_____
_____
_____
_____
_____
_____
_____
_____
_____
_____

Great quotes from this book:

Inspiration Tree

Why I read it?
_____
↓
It inspired me to
(read/learn/visit)?
_____
_____
↓
Who will I
recommend it to?
_____

✳ Ratings ✳

Plot: 1 2 3 4 5
Characters:
1 2 3 4 5
Ease of reading:
1 2 3 4 5
Overall
☹ 😐 🙂

68

Title:

Dates
Started: _____
Finished: _____

Source
Bought ○   Loaned ○
From: _____

Inspiration Tree

Why I read it?
_____
↓
It inspired me to
(read/learn/visit)?
_____
_____
↓
Who will I
recommend it to?
_____

✳ Ratings ✳

Plot: 1 2 3 4 5
Characters:
1 2 3 4 5
Ease of reading:
1 2 3 4 5
Overall
☹ 😐 🙂

Author: _____
Publisher: _____   Pub. date _____
Page count: _____
○ Fiction   ○ Non-fiction
  Genre: _____   Subject: _____

My Review:

_____
_____
_____
_____
_____
_____
_____
_____
_____
_____
_____
_____

Great quotes from this book:

Paperback ○   Hardback ○   e-book ○   Audiobook ○

69

Title:

Author: _____

Publisher: _____   Pub. date _____

Page count: _____

○ Fiction   ○ Non-fiction
   Genre: _____   Subject: _____

Dates
Started: _____
Finished: _____

Source
Bought ○ Loaned ○
From: _____

My Review: _____
_____
_____
_____
_____
_____
_____
_____
_____
_____
_____
_____
_____
_____
_____
_____

Great quotes from this book.

Inspiration Tree

Why I read it?
_____
⬇
It inspired me to
(read/learn/visit)?
_____
_____
⬇
Who will I
recommend it to?
_____

✳ Ratings ✳

Plot: 1 2 3 4 5
Characters:
1 2 3 4 5
Ease of reading:
1 2 3 4 5
Overall
☹ 😐 😊

70

Title:

Dates
Started: _____
Finished: _____

Source
Bought ○   Loaned ○
From: _____

💡

Inspiration Tree

Why I read it?
_____
⬇
It inspired me to
(read/learn/visit)?
_____
⬇
Who will I
recommend it to?
_____

✳ Ratings ✳

Plot: 1 2 3 4 5
Characters:
1 2 3 4 5
Ease of reading:
1 2 3 4 5
Overall
☹ 😐 🙂

Author: _____
Publisher: _____   Pub. date _____
Page count: _____
○ Fiction   ○ Non-fiction
   Genre: _____   Subject: _____

My Review:
_____
_____
_____
_____
_____
_____
_____
_____
_____
_____
_____
_____
_____
_____
_____
_____

Great quotes from this book:

Paperback ○   Hardback ○   e-book ○   Audiobook ○

71

Title:

Author: _____

Publisher: _____   Pub. date _____

Page count: _____

○ Fiction   ○ Non-fiction

Genre: _____   Subject: _____

Dates
Started: _____
Finished: _____

Source
Bought ○   Loaned ○
From: _____

My Review: _____
_____
_____
_____
_____
_____
_____
_____
_____
_____
_____
_____
_____

Inspiration Tree

Why I read it?
_____
⬇
It inspired me to
(read/learn/visit)?
_____
_____
⬇
Who will I
recommend it to?
_____

✳ Ratings ✳

Plot: 1 2 3 4 5
Characters:
1 2 3 4 5
Ease of reading:
1 2 3 4 5

Overall
☹ 😐 ☺

Great quotes from this book:

72

Title:

Dates
Started: _____
Finished: _____

Source
Bought ○ Loaned ○
From: _____

Author: _____
Publisher: _____ Pub. date _____
Page count: _____
○ Fiction   ○ Non-fiction
  Genre: _____   Subject: _____

💡
Inspiration Tree

Why I read it?
_____
↓
It inspired me to
(read/learn/visit)?
_____
_____
↓
Who will I
recommend it to?
_____

✳ Ratings ✳

Plot: 1 2 3 4 5
Characters:
1 2 3 4 5
Ease of reading:
1 2 3 4 5
Overall
☹ 😐 ☺

My Review:

_____
_____
_____
_____
_____
_____
_____
_____
_____
_____
_____
_____
_____
_____
_____

Great quotes from this book:

Paperback ○   Hardback ○   e-book ○   Audiobook ○

73

Title:

Author: _____

Publisher: _____ Pub. date _____

Page count. _____

○ Fiction   ○ Non-fiction
  Genre: _____   Subject: _____

Dates
Started: _____
Finished: _____

Source
Bought ○ Loaned ○
From: _____

My Review: _____
_____
_____
_____
_____
_____
_____
_____
_____
_____
_____
_____

Inspiration Tree

Why I read it?
_____

It inspired me to
(read/learn/visit)?
_____
_____

Who will I
recommend it to?
_____

✳ Ratings ✳

Plot: 1 2 3 4 5
Characters:
1 2 3 4 5
Ease of reading:
1 2 3 4 5
Overall

Great quotes from this book:

Paperback ○   Hardback ○   e-book ○   Audiobook ○

Title:

Dates
Started: _____
Finished: _____

Source
Bought ○ Loaned ○
From: _____

Author: _____
Publisher: _____ Pub. date _____
Page count: _____
○ Fiction   ○ Non-fiction
   Genre: _____   Subject: _____

My Review: _____
_____
_____
_____
_____
_____
_____
_____
_____
_____
_____
_____
_____
_____
_____

Inspiration Tree

Why I read it?
_____
↓
It inspired me to
(read/learn/visit)?
_____
↓
Who will I
recommend it to?
_____

✳ Ratings ✳

Plot: 1 2 3 4 5
Characters:
1 2 3 4 5
Ease of reading:
1 2 3 4 5
Overall
☹ 😐 ☺

Great quotes from this book:

Paperback ○   Hardback ○   e-book ○   Audiobook ○

75

Title:

Author: _____

Publisher: _____   Pub. date _____

Page count: _____

○ Fiction   ○ Non-fiction

   Genre: _____   Subject: _____

Dates
Started: _____
Finished: _____

Source
Bought ○   Loaned ○
From: _____

My Review: _____

_____

_____

_____

_____

_____

_____

_____

_____

_____

_____

_____

Inspiration Tree

Why I read it?
_____
↓
It inspired me to
(read/learn/visit)?
_____
_____
↓
Who will I
recommend it to?
_____

✳ Ratings ✳

Plot: 1 2 3 4 5

Characters:
1 2 3 4 5

Ease of reading:
1 2 3 4 5

Overall

Great quotes from this book:

76

Title:

Author: _____

Publisher: _____   Pub. date _____

Page count. _____

O Fiction   O Non-fiction

Genre: _____   Subject. _____

Dates

Started: _____

Finished: _____

Source

Bought O   Loaned O

From: _____

Inspiration Tree

Why I read it?

_____

⬇

It inspired me to
(read/learn/visit)?

_____

⬇

Who will I
recommend it to?

_____

✳ Ratings ✳

Plot. 1 2 3 4 5

Characters:

1 2 3 4 5

Ease of reading:

1 2 3 4 5

Overall

😞 😐 😊

My Review:

_____
_____
_____
_____
_____
_____
_____
_____
_____
_____
_____
_____
_____

Great quotes from this book:

Paperback ○   Hardback ○   e-book ○   Audiobook ○

Title:

Author:

Publisher: _____   Pub. date _____

Page count: _____

○ Fiction   ○ Non-fiction

   Genre: _____   Subject: _____

Dates
Started: _____
Finished: _____

Source
Bought ○   Loaned ○
From: _____

My Review: _____

_____

_____

_____

_____

_____

_____

_____

_____

_____

_____

_____

_____

Inspiration Tree

Why I read it?
_____

↓

It inspired me to
(read/learn/visit)?
_____

↓

Who will I
recommend it to?
_____

⋇ Ratings ⋇

Plot: 1 2 3 4 5
Characters:
1 2 3 4 5
Ease of reading:
1 2 3 4 5
Overall
☹ 😐 ☺

Great quotes from this book:

78

Title:

Author: _____

Publisher: _____   Pub. date _____

Page count: _____

○ Fiction   ○ Non-fiction

  Genre: _____   Subject: _____

Dates
Started: _____
Finished: _____

Source
Bought ○ Loaned ○
From: _____

Inspiration Tree

Why I read it?
_____
↓
It inspired me to
(read/learn/visit)?
_____
_____
↓
Who will I
recommend it to?
_____

※ Ratings ※

Plot: 1 2 3 4 5
Characters:
1 2 3 4 5
Ease of reading:
1 2 3 4 5
Overall
☹ 😐 🙂

My Review:

_____
_____
_____
_____
_____
_____
_____
_____
_____
_____
_____
_____
_____

Great quotes from this book:

Paperback ○   Hardback ○   e-book ○   Audiobook ○

79

Title:

Author: _____

Publisher: _____ Pub. date _____

Page count: _____

○ Fiction   ○ Non-fiction

  Genre: _____   Subject: _____

Dates
Started: _____
Finished: _____

Source
Bought ○ Loaned ○
From: _____

My Review: _____
_____
_____
_____
_____
_____
_____
_____
_____
_____
_____
_____
_____
_____

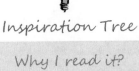

Inspiration Tree

Why I read it?
_____
↓
It inspired me to
(read/learn/visit)?
_____
_____
↓
Who will I
recommend it to?
_____

✳ Ratings ✳

Plot: 1 2 3 4 5
Characters:
1 2 3 4 5
Ease of reading:
1 2 3 4 5
Overall
☹ 😐 ☺

Great quotes from this book:

80

Title:

Dates
Started: _____
Finished: _____

Source
Bought ○ Loaned ○
From: _____

Author: _____
Publisher: _____ Pub. date _____
Page count: _____
○ Fiction   ○ Non-fiction
   Genre: _____   Subject: _____

Inspiration Tree

Why I read it?
_____
↓
It inspired me to
(read/learn/visit)?
_____
↓
Who will I
recommend it to?
_____

✳ Ratings ✳

Plot: 1 2 3 4 5
Characters:
1 2 3 4 5
Ease of reading:
1 2 3 4 5
Overall
☹ 😐 🙂

My Review:

_____
_____
_____
_____
_____
_____
_____
_____
_____
_____
_____
_____
_____
_____
_____

Great quotes from this book:

Paperback ○   Hardback ○   e-book ○   Audiobook ○

Title:

Author:

Publisher: _____   Pub. date _____

Page count: _____

○ Fiction   ○ Non-fiction

   Genre: _____   Subject: _____

Dates

Started: _____

Finished: _____

Source

Bought ○ Loaned ○

From: _____

My Review: _____

_____

_____

_____

_____

_____

_____

_____

_____

_____

_____

_____

Inspiration Tree

Why I read it?

_____

⬇

It inspired me to
(read/learn/visit)?

_____

_____

⬇

Who will I
recommend it to?

_____

✳ Ratings ✳

Plot: 1 2 3 4 5

Characters:
1 2 3 4 5

Ease of reading:
1 2 3 4 5

Overall

☹ 😐 ☺

Great quotes from this book:

Paperback ○   Hardback ○   e-book ○   Audiobook ○

Title:

Dates
Started: _____
Finished: _____

Source
Bought ○   Loaned ○
From: _____

Author: _____

Publisher: _____   Pub. date _____

Page count: _____

○ Fiction   ○ Non-fiction
  Genre: _____   Subject: _____

Inspiration Tree

Why I read it?
_____
↓
It inspired me to
(read/learn/visit)?
_____
↓
Who will I
recommend it to?
_____

My Review:
_____
_____
_____
_____
_____
_____
_____
_____
_____
_____
_____
_____
_____
_____

✳ Ratings ✳

Plot: 1 2 3 4 5

Characters:
1 2 3 4 5

Ease of reading:
1 2 3 4 5

Overall
☹ 😐 🙂

Great quotes from this book:

Paperback ○　　Hardback ○　　e-book ○　　Audiobook ○

Title:

Author: _____

Publisher: _____　　Pub. date _____

Page count: _____

○ Fiction　　　　　　　　○ Non-fiction

Genre: _____　　Subject: _____

Dates
Started: _____
Finished: _____

Source
Bought ○　Loaned ○
From: _____

My Review: _____

_____

_____

_____

_____

_____

_____

_____

_____

_____

Inspiration Tree

Why I read it?
_____
↓
It inspired me to
(read/learn/visit)?
_____
_____
↓
Who will I
recommend it to?
_____

Great quotes from this book:

✳ Ratings ✳

Plot: 1 2 3 4 5

Characters:
1 2 3 4 5

Ease of reading:
1 2 3 4 5

Overall

84

Title:

Author: _____

Publisher: _____   Pub. date _____

Page count: _____

○ Fiction   ○ Non-fiction

  Genre: _____   Subject: _____

Dates

Started: _____

Finished: _____

Source

Bought ○   Loaned ○

From: _____

💡

Inspiration Tree

Why I read it?

_____

⬇

It inspired me to
(read/learn/visit)?

_____

_____

⬇

Who will I
recommend it to?

_____

✵ Ratings ✵

Plot: 1 2 3 4 5

Characters:
1 2 3 4 5

Ease of reading:
1 2 3 4 5

Overall

☹ 😐 ☺

My Review:

_____
_____
_____
_____
_____
_____
_____
_____
_____
_____
_____
_____
_____

Great quotes from this book:

Paperback ○   Hardback ○   e-book ○   Audiobook ○

85

Title:

Author: _____

Publisher: _____ Pub. date _____

Page count: _____

○ Fiction   ○ Non-fiction
   Genre: _____   Subject: _____

Dates
Started: _____
Finished: _____

Source
Bought ○   Loaned ○
From: _____

My Review: _____

_____

_____

_____

_____

_____

_____

_____

_____

_____

_____

_____

Great quotes from this book:

Inspiration Tree

Why I read it?
_____

It inspired me to
(read/learn/visit)?
_____
_____

Who will I
recommend it to?
_____

⁂ Ratings ⁂

Plot: 1 2 3 4 5
Characters:
1 2 3 4 5
Ease of reading:
1 2 3 4 5
Overall
☹ 😐 ☺

Paperback ○   Hardback ○   e-book ○   Audiobook ○

Title:

Author: _____

Publisher: _____   Pub. date _____

Page count: _____

○ Fiction   ○ Non-fiction
  Genre: _____   Subject: _____

Dates
Started: _____
Finished: _____

Source
Bought ○   Loaned ○
From: _____

Inspiration Tree

Why I read it?
_____
↓
It inspired me to
(read/learn/visit)?
_____
_____
↓
Who will I
recommend it to?
_____

✳ Ratings ✳

Plot: 1 2 3 4 5
Characters:
1 2 3 4 5
Ease of reading:
1 2 3 4 5
Overall
☹ 😐 ☺

My Review:

_____
_____
_____
_____
_____
_____
_____
_____
_____
_____
_____
_____

Great quotes from this book:

Paperback ○   Hardback ○   e-book ○   Audiobook ○

87

Title:

Author: _____

Publisher: _____   Pub. date _____

Page count: _____

○ Fiction   ○ Non-fiction

   Genre: _____   Subject: _____

Dates
Started: _____
Finished: _____

Source
Bought ○ Loaned ○
From: _____

My Review: _____

_____

_____

_____

_____

_____

_____

_____

_____

_____

_____

_____

_____

Inspiration Tree

Why I read it?
_____
↓
It inspired me to
(read/learn/visit)?
_____
_____
↓
Who will I
recommend it to?
_____

Great quotes from this book:

✳ Ratings ✳

Plot: 1 2 3 4 5

Characters:
1 2 3 4 5

Ease of reading:
1 2 3 4 5

Overall

88

Title:

Dates
Started: _____
Finished: _____

Source
Bought ○   Loaned ○
From: _____

Author: _____
Publisher: _____   Pub. date _____
Page count: _____
○ Fiction   ○ Non-fiction
   Genre: _____   Subject: _____

My Review:
_____
_____
_____
_____
_____
_____
_____
_____
_____
_____
_____
_____
_____
_____

💡

Inspiration Tree

Why I read it?
_____
⬇
It inspired me to
(read/learn/visit)?
_____
_____
⬇
Who will I
recommend it to?
_____

✳ Ratings ✳

Plot: 1 2 3 4 5
Characters:
1 2 3 4 5
Ease of reading:
1 2 3 4 5
Overall
☹ 😐 ☺

Great quotes from this book:

Paperback ○   Hardback ○   e-book ○   Audiobook ○

89

Title:

Author:
Publisher: Pub. date
Page count:
○ Fiction   ○ Non-fiction
   Genre: Subject:

Dates
Started: _____
Finished: _____

Source
Bought ○ Loaned ○
From: _____

My Review:
_____
_____
_____
_____
_____
_____
_____
_____
_____
_____
_____
_____

Inspiration Tree

Why I read it?
_____
↓
It inspired me to
(read/learn/visit)?
_____
↓
Who will I
recommend it to?
_____

✳ Ratings ✳

Plot: 1 2 3 4 5
Characters:
1 2 3 4 5
Ease of reading:
1 2 3 4 5
Overall
☹ 😐 ☺

Great quotes from this book:

Paperback ○   Hardback ○   e-book ○   Audiobook ○

Title:

Dates
Started: _____
Finished: _____

Source
Bought ○ Loaned ○
From: _____

Author: _____
Publisher: _____ Pub. date _____
Page count: _____
○ Fiction   ○ Non-fiction
  Genre: _____   Subject: _____

Inspiration Tree

Why I read it?
_____
↓
It inspired me to
(read/learn/visit)?
_____
↓
Who will I
recommend it to?
_____

✳ Ratings ✳

Plot: 1 2 3 4 5
Characters:
1 2 3 4 5
Ease of reading:
1 2 3 4 5
Overall
☹ 😐 🙂

My Review:

_____
_____
_____
_____
_____
_____
_____
_____
_____
_____
_____
_____
_____
_____

Great quotes from this book:

Paperback ○   Hardback ○   e-book ○   Audiobook ○

Title:

Author: _____

Publisher: _____   Pub. date _____

Page count: _____

○ Fiction   ○ Non-fiction
   Genre: _____   Subject: _____

Dates
Started: _____
Finished: _____

Source
Bought ○   Loaned ○

From: _____

My Review: _____
_____
_____
_____
_____
_____
_____
_____
_____
_____
_____
_____
_____

Inspiration Tree

Why I read it?
_____
⬇
It inspired me to
(read/learn/visit)?
_____
_____
⬇
Who will I
recommend it to?
_____

✳ Ratings ✳

Plot: 1 2 3 4 5
Characters:
1 2 3 4 5
Ease of reading:
1 2 3 4 5

Overall

Great quotes from this book:

Paperback ○   Hardback ○   e-book ○   Audiobook ○

Title:

Dates
Started: _____
Finished: _____

Source
Bought ○ Loaned ○
From: _____

💡

Inspiration Tree

Why I read it?
_____
⬇
It inspired me to
(read/learn/visit)?
_____
⬇
Who will I
recommend it to?
_____

✳ Ratings ✳

Plot: 1 2 3 4 5
Characters:
1 2 3 4 5
Ease of reading:
1 2 3 4 5
Overall
☹ 😐 🙂

Author: _____
Publisher: _____   Pub. date _____
Page count: _____
○ Fiction   ○ Non-fiction
   Genre: _____   Subject: _____

My Review:
_____
_____
_____
_____
_____
_____
_____
_____
_____
_____
_____
_____
_____
_____

Great quotes from this book:

Paperback ○   Hardback ○   e-book ○   Audiobook ○

93

Title:

Author:
Publisher: Pub. date
Page count:
○ Fiction   ○ Non-fiction
   Genre: Subject:

Dates
Started:
Finished:

Source
Bought ○   Loaned ○
From:

My Review:

Inspiration Tree

Why I read it?

It inspired me to
(read/learn/visit)?

Who will I
recommend it to?

✳ Ratings ✳

Plot: 1 2 3 4 5
Characters:
1 2 3 4 5
Ease of reading:
1 2 3 4 5
Overall
☹ 😐 ☺

Great quotes from this book:

94

Title:

Dates
Started: _____
Finished: _____

Source
Bought ○   Loaned ○
From: _____

Author: _____

Publisher: _____   Pub. date _____

Page count: _____

○ Fiction   ○ Non-fiction
   Genre: _____   Subject: _____

💡

Inspiration Tree

Why I read it?
_____
⬇
It inspired me to
(read/learn/visit)?
_____
_____
⬇
Who will I
recommend it to?
_____

My Review:

_____
_____
_____
_____
_____
_____
_____
_____
_____
_____
_____
_____
_____
_____
_____

✳ Ratings ✳

Plot: 1 2 3 4 5
Characters:
1 2 3 4 5
Ease of reading:
1 2 3 4 5
Overall
☹ 😐 🙂

Great quotes from this book:

Paperback ○   Hardback ○   e-book ○   Audiobook ○

95

Title:

Author: _____

Publisher: _____   Pub. date _____

Page count: _____

○ Fiction   ○ Non-fiction

Genre: _____   Subject: _____

Source
Bought ○   Loaned ○
From: _____

My Review: _____

_____

_____

_____

_____

_____

_____

_____

_____

_____

_____

Inspiration Tree

Why I read it?
_____
⬇
It inspired me to
(read/learn/visit)?
_____
_____
⬇
Who will I
recommend it to?
_____

✳ Ratings ✳

Plot: 1 2 3 4 5

Characters:
1 2 3 4 5

Ease of reading:
1 2 3 4 5

Overall
☹ 😐 🙂

Great quotes from this book:

Paperback ○   Hardback ○   e-book ○   Audiobook ○

Title:

Dates
Started: _____
Finished: _____

Source
Bought ○   Loaned ○
From: _____

Author: _____

Publisher: _____   Pub. date _____

Page count: _____

○ Fiction
   Genre: _____

○ Non-fiction
   Subject: _____

My Review:

_____
_____
_____
_____
_____
_____
_____
_____
_____
_____
_____
_____
_____
_____
_____

Inspiration Tree

Why I read it?
_____
↓
It inspired me to
(read/learn/visit)?
_____
↓
Who will I
recommend it to?
_____

✳ Ratings ✳

Plot: 1 2 3 4 5

Characters:
1 2 3 4 5

Ease of reading:
1 2 3 4 5

Overall
☹ 😐 🙂

Great quotes from this book:

Paperback ○   Hardback ○   e-book ○   Audiobook ○

97

Title:

Author: _____

Publisher: _____ Pub. date _____

Page count: _____

○ Fiction   ○ Non-fiction
  Genre: _____   Subject: _____

Dates
Started: _____
Finished: _____

Source
Bought ○   Loaned ○
From: _____

My Review: _____
_____
_____
_____
_____
_____
_____
_____
_____
_____
_____
_____
_____
_____

Inspiration Tree

Why I read it?
_____
⬇
It inspired me to
(read/learn/visit)?
_____
⬇
Who will I
recommend it to?
_____

✳ Ratings ✳

Plot: 1 2 3 4 5
Characters:
1 2 3 4 5
Ease of reading:
1 2 3 4 5
Overall
☹ 😐 ☺

Great quotes from this book:

98

Title:

Dates
Started: _____
Finished: _____

Source
Bought ○   Loaned ○
From: _____

Author: _____

Publisher: _____   Pub. date _____

Page count: _____

○ Fiction   ○ Non-fiction
  Genre: _____   Subject: _____

Inspiration Tree

Why I read it?
_____
⬇
It inspired me to
(read/learn/visit)?
_____
_____
⬇
Who will I
recommend it to?
_____

✳ Ratings ✳

Plot: 1 2 3 4 5
Characters:
1 2 3 4 5
Ease of reading:
1 2 3 4 5
Overall
☹ 😐 😊

My Review:

_____
_____
_____
_____
_____
_____
_____
_____
_____
_____
_____
_____
_____

Great quotes from this book:

Paperback ○   Hardback ○   e-book ○   Audiobook ○

99

Title:

Author: _____

Publisher: _____   Pub. date _____

Page count: _____

○ Fiction   ○ Non-fiction

Genre: _____   Subject: _____

Dates
Started: _____
Finished: _____

Source
Bought ○   Loaned ○

From: _____

My Review: _____

_____

_____

_____

_____

_____

_____

_____

_____

_____

_____

_____

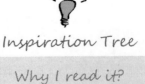

Inspiration Tree

Why I read it?
_____
⬇
It inspired me to
(read/learn/visit)?
_____
_____
⬇
Who will I
recommend it to?
_____

✳ Ratings ✳

Plot: 1 2 3 4 5

Characters:
1 2 3 4 5

Ease of reading:
1 2 3 4 5

Overall
☹ 😐 ☺

Great quotes from this book:

100

Title:

Dates
Started: _____
Finished: _____

Source
Bought ○   Loaned ○
From: _____

💡

Inspiration Tree

Why I read it?
_____
⬇
It inspired me to
(read/learn/visit)?
_____
_____
⬇
Who will I
recommend it to?
_____

✳ Ratings ✳

Plot: 1 2 3 4 5
Characters:
1 2 3 4 5
Ease of reading:
1 2 3 4 5
Overall
☹ 😐 ☺

Author: _____
Publisher: _____   Pub. date _____
Page count: _____
○ Fiction   ○ Non-fiction
  Genre: _____   Subject: _____

My Review: _____
_____
_____
_____
_____
_____
_____
_____
_____
_____
_____
_____
_____

Great quotes from this book:

The Big Read

Top 100 Voted Fiction Books

- 1. The Lord of the Rings, JRR Tolkien
- 2. Pride and Prejudice, Jane Austen
- 3. His Dark Materials, Philip Pullman
- 4. The Hitchhiker's Guide to the Galaxy, Douglas Adams
- 5. Harry Potter and the Goblet of Fire, JK Rowling
- 6. To Kill a Mockingbird, Harper Lee
- 7. Winnie the Pooh, AA Milne
- 8. Nineteen Eighty-Four, George Orwell
- 9. The Lion, the Witch and the Wardrobe, CS Lewis
- 10. Jane Eyre, Charlotte Brontë
- 11. Catch-22, Joseph Heller
- 12. Wuthering Heights, Emily Brontë
- 13. Birdsong, Sebastian Faulks
- 14. Rebecca, Daphne du Maurier
- 15. The Catcher in the Rye, JD Salinger
- 16. The Wind in the Willows, Kenneth Grahame
- 17. Great Expectations, Charles Dickens
- 18. Little Women, Louisa May Alcott
- 19. Captain Corelli's Mandolin, Louis de Bernieres
- 20. War and Peace, Leo Tolstoy
- 21. Gone with the Wind, Margaret Mitchell
- 22. Harry Potter And The Philosopher's Stone, JK Rowling
- 23. Harry Potter And The Chamber Of Secrets, JK Rowling
- 24. Harry Potter And The Prisoner Of Azkaban, JK Rowling
- 25. The Hobbit, JRR Tolkien
- 26. Tess Of The D'Urbervilles, Thomas Hardy
- 27. Middlemarch, George Eliot
- 28. A Prayer For Owen Meany, John Irving
- 29. The Grapes Of Wrath, John Steinbeck
- 30. Alice's Adventures In Wonderland, Lewis Carroll

- 31. The Story Of Tracy Beaker, Jacqueline Wilson
- 32. One Hundred Years Of Solitude, Gabriel García Márquez
- 33. The Pillars Of The Earth, Ken Follett
- 34. David Copperfield, Charles Dickens
- 35. Charlie And The Chocolate Factory, Roald Dahl
- 36. Treasure Island, Robert Louis Stevenson
- 37. A Town Like Alice, Nevil Shute
- 38. Persuasion, Jane Austen
- 39. Dune, Frank Herbert
- 40. Emma, Jane Austen
- 41. Anne Of Green Gables, LM Montgomery
- 42. Watership Down, Richard Adams
- 43. The Great Gatsby, F Scott Fitzgerald
- 44. The Count Of Monte Cristo, Alexandre Dumas
- 45. Brideshead Revisited, Evelyn Waugh
- 46. Animal Farm, George Orwell
- 47. A Christmas Carol, Charles Dickens
- 48. Far From The Madding Crowd, Thomas Hardy
- 49. Goodnight Mister Tom, Michelle Magorian
- 50. The Shell Seekers, Rosamunde Pilc
- 51. The Secret Garden, Frances Hodgson Burnett
- 52. Of Mice And Men, John Steinbeck
- 53. The Stand, Stephen King
- 54. Anna Karenina, Leo Tolstoy
- 55. A Suitable Boy, Vikram Seth
- 56. The BFG, Roald Dahl
- 57. Swallows And Amazons, Arthur Ransome
- 58. Black Beauty, Anna Sewell
- 59. Artemis Fowl, Eoin Colfer
- 60. Crime And Punishment, Fyodor Dostoyevsky
- 61. Noughts And Crosses, Malorie Blackman
- 62. Memoirs Of A Geisha, Arthur Golden
- 63. A Tale Of Two Cities, Charles Dickens
- 64. The Thorn Birds, Colleen McCollough
- 65. Mort, Terry Pratchett

- 66. The Magic Faraway Tree, Enid Blyton
- 67. The Magus, John Fowles
- 68. Good Omens, Terry Pratchett and Neil Gaiman
- 69. Guards! Guards!, Terry Pratchett
- 70. Lord Of The Flies, William Golding
- 71. Perfume, Patrick Süskind
- 72. The Ragged Trousered Philanthropists, Robert Tressell
- 73. Night Watch, Terry Pratchett
- 74. Matilda, Roald Dahl
- 75. Bridget Jones's Diary, Helen Fielding
- 76. The Secret History, Donna Tartt
- 77. The Woman In White, Wilkie Collins
- 78. Ulysses, James Joyce
- 79. Bleak House, Charles Dickens
- 80. Double Act, Jacqueline Wilson
- 81. The Twits, Roald Dahl
- 82. I Capture The Castle, Dodie Smith
- 83. Holes, Louis Sachar
- 84. Gormenghast, Mervyn Peake
- 85. The God Of Small Things, Arundhati Roy
- 86. Vicky Angel, Jacqueline Wilson
- 87. Brave New World, Aldous Huxley
- 88. Cold Comfort Farm, Stella Gibbons
- 89. Magician, Raymond E Feist
- 90. On The Road, Jack Kerouac
- 91. The Godfather, Mario Puzo
- 92. The Clan Of The Cave Bear, Jean M Auel
- 93. The Colour Of Magic, Terry Pratchett
- 94. The Alchemist, Paulo Coelho
- 95. Katherine, Anya Seton
- 96. Kane And Abel, Jeffrey Archer
- 97. Love In The Time Of Cholera, Gabriel García Márquez
- 98. Girls In Love, Jacqueline Wilson
- 99. The Princess Diaries, Meg Cabot
- 100. Midnight's Children, Salman Rushdie

Notes: (books to read, new authors, book supplier's contact details, reading resources etc.)

Loan Record

Book	Borrowed from	Leant to	Date Borrowed	Date Returned

Made in the USA
San Bernardino, CA
07 August 2018